MASTERING THE DIGITAL CHESSBOARD

Mastering Chess in the Digital Age

John Dollar

Table of Contents

INTRODUCTION

In the heart of a bustling city, resonating with the rhythmic hum of technology, lived Alex Mercer, a young prodigy with a passion for chess. His eyes sparkled with insatiable curiosity and his nimble fingers danced across the keys of the sleek laptop. The digital chessboard was his battlefield and he was determined to conquer it.

Alex's journey began when he came across an online chess platform where players from all over the world faced off in virtual matches. Preoccupied, he plunged headfirst into the realm of 64 fields and endless possibilities.

His first opponent, an anonymous player nicknamed "SilentKnight", greeted him with a snide "Good luck". Undeterred, Alex conducted his compositions like a master conducting a symphony. He quickly realized that the digital battlefield required a different skill set, strategic foresight, adaptability, and lightning-fast decision-making.

As the game progressed, Alex found himself in a precarious position. SilentKnight's movements were unpredictable and the pressure was building every moment. But Alex accepted the challenge and made use of the vast ocean of chess strategies he had studied. His fingers moved with purpose, each movement a calculated move to victory.

In the end, Alex came out victorious, but he knew this was just the beginning. The excitement of the digital chessboard lit a fire in him and made him explore the nuances of the online game.

With each victory, Alex gained both supporters and opponents. The digital chess community was buzzing with whispers about a child prodigy who seemed to have an uncanny knack for predicting the moves of his opponents. Some hailed him as a genius, while others speculated about the secrets of his success.

To unravel the mysteries of the digital chessboard, Alex delved into the world of chess engines and artificial intelligence. He spent countless hours studying the algorithms that powered these digital adversaries, determined to master their secrets. The lines between man and machine blurred as he honed his skills and drew inspiration from both worlds.

As Alex continued to climb, he ran into players pushing him to the brink of defeat. Each loss became a valuable lesson, a stepping stone on his way to the championship. He dissected his plays, analyzed his mistakes and adjusted his strategies. The digital chessboard became a canvas for his growth, a space where he painted his victories and learned from his defeats.

One day, a formidable opponent named QuantumMind challenged Alex to a match. The chessboard seemed to pulse with energy as the two minds clashed in a battle of wits. QuantumMind's moves were calculated and precise, pushing Alex to the limits of his strategic prowess.

The match unfolded like a tense drama, every move increasing the tension. Viewers from around the world tuned in to witness the clash of the titans. The chat was flooded with messages of anticipation, with fans and skeptics alike wondering if Alex could maintain his unbeaten streak.

In the end, after a grueling battle that mentally drained both players, Alex emerged victorious. The chessboard witnessed a masterpiece, a symphony of moves that left the spectators in awe. QuantumMind graciously recognized Alex's skill, and the digital chess community erupted in applause.

Alex's journey to the digital chessboard has come full circle. From a curious novice to a seasoned master, he conquered the virtual realm. But instead of basking in the glory, he humbly acknowledged the endless possibilities that still lay before him. The digital chessboard was constantly evolving and Alex was ready to face new challenges, armed with the wisdom gained from every move, every victory and every defeat.

Mastering the digital chessboard is a journey that transcends the traditional boundaries of the game. In an era dominated by technology, the chessboard has moved from the physical to the digital realm, opening up a new dimension for players to explore and conquer. This transformation brings with it unique challenges and opportunities, requiring a new approach to understanding and excelling in the game.

When delving into the complexities of controlling a digital chessboard, it is essential to recognize a fundamental shift in dynamics. The tactile sensation of moving wooden pieces is replaced by the click of a mouse, and face-to-face battles become online battles against opponents from around the world. Once limited to living rooms and park tables, chess is now expanding its boundaries through online platforms and sophisticated software.

One of the key aspects of navigating this digital landscape is knowing the various online chess platforms. Each platform has its own interface, features and community. From the elegant simplicity of Chess.com to the sophisticated analytical tools of lichess.org, players must adapt to the nuances of these platforms to optimize their learning and playing experiences. Understanding how to use features such as puzzles, lessons, and game analysis tools becomes essential to mastering skills in this digital arena.

In addition, mastering the digital chessboard requires an appreciation for the vast databases and engines that have become an integral part of the current game. Chess engines like Stockfish and Komodo have evolved into powerful companions that provide real-time analysis and insights. Learning to harness the potential of these engines can improve understanding of positions, tactics and strategic nuances. The ability to critically evaluate the suggestions generated by the engine becomes a skill in itself as players walk the fine line between relying on artificial intelligence and applying their own intuition.

In this digital age, the availability of vast databases offers gamers an unprecedented opportunity to study and learn from both historical and contemporary games. Analyzing the games of grandmasters and understanding their thought processes provides invaluable insights. Digital Realm provides easy access to a huge repository of games, allowing players to explore different openings, study complex endgames, and witness the evolution of chess strategies over time. Skillful use of these databases can greatly accelerate the learning curve, allowing players to stand on the shoulders of giants.

An often underestimated aspect of mastering the digital board is developing a robust online presence. Building an online chess profile involves more than just collecting a high rating; requires consistent participation in the online chess community. Participating in forums, joining clubs and participating in tournaments contributes to the growth of a player off the board. The social aspect of online chess brings a new level of complexity, where sportsmanship, etiquette and communication skills play a vital role in creating a positive and rewarding experience for yourself and other players.

Digital Chessboard also features a variety of training tools and resources tailored to individual needs and skill levels. Interactive lessons, tactics coaches and specialized courses are designed for both beginners and advanced players. The customization options available in the digital realm allow players to focus on specific areas of improvement, whether it's opening theory, understanding position, or mastering the endgame. The ability to prepare an individual training regimen is a great advantage that digital platforms offer to those who want to reach new heights in their chess journey.

As we navigate the complexities of the digital chessboard, it is essential to acknowledge the impact of online chess communities on the learning process. Interacting with other enthusiasts, discussing strategies and seeking advice contribute to a common pool of knowledge. The global nature of online chess communities exposes players to a variety of play styles and strategies and encourages adaptability and resilience. Collaborative learning becomes a cornerstone as players share insights, analyze games together, and work together to improve.

Beyond the competitive aspect, the digital chessboard serves as a canvas for creativity and innovation. The integration of variants such as Fischer Random Chess and 3-check brings new challenges and pushes players to think outside of conventional boundaries. Online platforms also host themed tournaments where players explore specific openings or themes in a dynamic and engaging environment. Embracing these creative dimensions adds depth to the understanding of the game and promotes a holistic approach to chess mastery.

In the digital realm, the traditional division between casual play and serious competition is becoming fluid. Casual games seamlessly transition into intense battles with highly skilled opponents, blurring the lines

Chapter 1 Understanding Digital Chess

Chess, a timeless game that has evolved over centuries, has embraced the digital age with the advent of digital chess boards. In this era of technological advancement, the traditional wooden chessboard has transformed into a digital interface that opens up new dimensions for players and enthusiasts. This article delves into the nuances of understanding digital chess and explores strategies for mastering the digital chessboard.

The evolution of chess in the digital realm

A paradigm shift:
The transition from physical to digital chess boards represents a paradigm shift in the way chess is played and learned. Digital chess platforms offer countless advantages, including accessibility,

convenience, and the ability to connect with opponents from around the world. Players can join matches, analyze games and access an extensive database of openings and tactics with just a few clicks.

Accessibility and inclusivity:
One of the remarkable aspects of digital chess is its accessibility. Players no longer need a physical opponent; they can challenge the computer on different difficulty levels or play against opponents online. This inclusivity has contributed to the popularity of the game as enthusiasts of all skill levels can participate and improve their game.

Mastering the Digital Chessboard: Strategies and Techniques

Use of online educational resources
Digital platforms provide a treasure trove of educational resources for chess enthusiasts. From tutorials and interactive lessons to grandmaster analysis, players can use these resources to better understand the game. Online chess courses and

webinars offer structured learning paths that are suitable for both beginners and advanced players.

Analysis of games using chess engines:
Chess engines have revolutionized the way players analyze games. These powerful programs can evaluate positions, suggest optimal moves and point out mistakes. By incorporating chess engines into their practice routine, players can gain insight into their strengths and weaknesses and ultimately improve their skills and decision making.

Virtual tournaments and competitive games:
The digital realm gave rise to virtual chess tournaments that gave players the opportunity to test their skills against a diverse field of competitors. Participating in online competitions increases a player's ability to handle pressure, adapt to different play styles, and hone strategic thinking. Virtual tournaments also contribute to the growth of the online chess community and foster a sense of camaraderie among players around the world.

Technical challenges

While digital chess offers a number of advantages, players may encounter technical issues such as connectivity issues, software glitches, or hardware limitations. It is crucial for players to address these challenges to ensure a seamless gaming experience and focus on improving their skills without unnecessary disruption.

Balancing digital and traditional chess:

As digital chess grows in importance, players must find a balance between digital and traditional forms of play. The tactile sensation of physical chess pieces and face-to-face interaction can offer a different kind of experience that complements the digital realm. Achieving this balance ensures a versatile approach to chess mastery.

The future of digital chess

Artificial Intelligence and Machine Learning:

The integration of artificial intelligence (AI) and machine learning (ML) in digital chess is shaping the future of the game. Advanced algorithms are constantly evolving and challenge even the most experienced players. Understanding and adapting to these technological advances will be essential for players who want to reach the pinnacle of chess mastery.

Virtual reality chess.

The emergence of virtual reality (VR) in chess brings a new dimension to the game. VR platforms can simulate the experience of playing on a physical board, enhancing immersion and providing a unique combination of traditional and digital elements. Exploring the possibilities of VR chess can become an exciting avenue for players looking for new ways to engage with the game.

Understanding digital chess involves embracing the opportunities that the digital board offers while also being aware of the challenges it presents. Mastering the digital chessboard requires a strategic approach, using online resources, analyzing games using chess engines, and actively participating in virtual tournaments. As the chess community continues to evolve in the digital era, players must adapt and use technology to improve their skills and stay at the forefront of this timeless game. Whether you prefer the traditional wooden board or the clicking of digital pieces, the essence of chess remains: a battle of wits, strategy and constant improvement.

1.1 Overview of Digital Chess Platforms

Digital chess platforms have revolutionized the way enthusiasts engage in the timeless game of chess, providing a dynamic and immersive environment for players of all skill levels. As technology continues to advance, these platforms offer a plethora of features that contribute to mastering the digital chessboard.

One of the key aspects of digital chess platforms is their accessibility. Unlike traditional overboard gaming, players can access these platforms from the comfort of their homes, allowing them to engage in matches against opponents from around the world. This accessibility promotes a diverse and challenging playing field and exposes individuals to different play styles and strategies.

In addition, digital chess platforms often include sophisticated matchmaking algorithms that match players based on their skill level. This ensures a balanced and competitive experience that allows users to gradually improve their skills. Being able to face opponents of similar expertise is crucial to improvement as it presents an opportunity to learn from each game and adapt strategies accordingly.

The digital environment also facilitates continuous learning through features such as computer analysis. Many platforms offer real-time game analysis and provide insight into moves, mistakes and alternative strategies. This analysis tool serves as a valuable advisor to help players understand the rationale behind certain moves and refine their thought processes during the game.

In addition, digital platforms often include extensive tutorials and lessons for players of various skill levels. From the basics for beginners to advanced tactics, these resources allow users to better understand chess principles. Interactive lessons, puzzles and exercises contribute to a comprehensive learning experience and create a solid foundation for mastering the complexities of the digital chessboard.

Another notable aspect is the extensive community aspect of digital chess platforms. Players can participate in forums, participate in discussions and engage with chess enthusiasts around the world. This sense of community fosters the exchange of knowledge, strategies and experiences and creates a supportive environment for players looking to raise their game. Learning from others, sharing insights, and discussing game analysis contribute significantly to the overall learning process.

The rise of artificial intelligence (AI) has also had a profound impact on digital chess platforms. Many platforms integrate AI-powered engines that players can compete with or use for analysis. Playing against a computer opponent with adjustable difficulty levels allows users to fine-tune their skills and experiment with different strategies. The analytical capabilities of the AI engines serve as a formidable tool for players who want to understand the intricacies of different positions and improve their decision-making skills.

In addition, digital chess platforms offer a wide variety of time controls, from quick and blitz to classic time formats. This variety allows players to develop adaptability and expertise at different game tempos. Mastering the digital chessboard requires not only strategic thinking, but also the ability to manage time effectively, and these platforms provide the perfect arena for honing this key skill.

An often underappreciated feature of digital chess platforms is the convenience of reviewing past games. Players can revisit their matches, analyze critical positions and identify patterns in their play. This retrospective approach allows for continuous self-improvement as individuals can learn from their mistakes and utilize successful strategies. The ability to maintain a personal database of games serves as a valuable resource for tracking progress and identifying areas that require further attention.

In addition, digital platforms often organize online tournaments that provide players with the opportunity to test their skills in a competitive environment. These tournaments attract participants from a variety of backgrounds and skill levels and offer a challenging yet rewarding experience. The competitive aspect of tournaments encourages growth of the mind and encourages players to learn from both wins and losses.

Digital chess platforms have proven to be indispensable tools for mastering the digital chessboard. The accessibility, analytical capabilities, diverse community, and learning resources offered by these platforms contribute to a holistic and immersive chess experience. Whether you are a beginner struggling to understand the basics or an experienced player aspiring to mastery, the digital chess landscape provides an ever-evolving and enriching environment to hone your skills and enjoy the timeless game of chess.

1.2 Advantages and Challenges of Online Chess

Online chess has become a pivotal platform for enthusiasts and professionals alike, offering countless advantages and unique challenges in the pursuit of mastering the digital chessboard. As technology continues to reshape the landscape of traditional board games, online chess presents both opportunities and obstacles for players to overcome.

One of the main advantages of online chess is its accessibility. Players from all over the world can join matches at any time, break down geographical barriers and support a diverse and vibrant community. The ability to team up with opponents of varying skill levels improves learning opportunities and allows players to face a wide variety of strategies and styles. This exposure significantly contributes to the development of skills, promotes adaptability and strategic thinking.

The digital platform also provides a large number of learning resources. Online tutorials, chess databases, and analytical tools allow players to independently study and improve their game. The availability of countless instructional videos and commented games from grandmasters offers invaluable insights that make the learning process more dynamic and engaging. This vast repository of knowledge accelerates skill acquisition and deepens understanding, creating a rich learning environment for players looking to master the intricacies of the game.

In addition, online chess platforms often include features such as computer analysis and game statistics. These tools offer instant feedback on moves, highlighting mistakes and suggesting improvements. This real-time analysis supports a continuous learning cycle that allows players to identify weaknesses and refine their strategies. The analytical aspect of online chess increases self-awareness and accelerates improvement, creating a more efficient path to mastery.

Despite these advantages, the digital realm presents its own set of challenges for novice chess players. One significant obstacle is the possibility of cheating. The anonymity provided by online play may tempt some players to use chess engines or external help, which undermines the integrity of the game. Online platforms use anti-cheating measures, but the constant cat-and-mouse game between developers and fraudsters remains a constant challenge.

Another problem is the lack of physical presence. Traditional chess involves sitting across from your opponent, observing their body language and tangibly experiencing the intensity of the game. Online play replaces this with a virtual interface that potentially weakens the emotional and psychological aspects of the game. Mastering the digital board requires players to adapt to this shift and focus on virtual elements that convey the essence of the game without physical presence.

Time management is becoming a crucial aspect of online chess. While traditional chess tournaments have a set time control, online platforms offer a plethora of options, from blitz to correspondence games. Managing the clock effectively is a skill in itself, and the fast pace of online gaming requires quick thinking and decisive movements. Learning to balance speed and accuracy is paramount for those seeking mastery in the digital chess arena.

An additional challenge is the occurrence of distractions in the online environment. Unlike a board game where players are immersed in a controlled environment, online chess can be prone to interruptions and external stimuli. Mastering the digital chessboard requires discipline and the ability to maintain focus even in the face of potential interruptions, ensuring a consistent, high-quality gaming experience.

The journey to mastering the digital chessboard through online play is a dynamic and rewarding endeavor. The accessibility, learning resources and analytical tools offered by online platforms create a fertile ground for skill development. However, players must navigate challenges such as the risks of cheating, the absence of a physical presence, time management, and potential distractions. Achieving a balance between taking advantage and overcoming challenges is essential for those who want to reach the pinnacle of online chess mastery.

1.3 Importance of Digital Chess in Skill Development

In an era dominated by technological advancements, traditional board games have found a new digital dimension, and chess is no exception. The transition from physical chessboards to their digital counterparts has not only revolutionized the way we play, but has also brought countless benefits in terms of skill development. As more and more hobbyists and professionals alike turn to digital platforms for their chess endeavors, the importance of mastering a digital chessboard is becoming increasingly apparent.

1. Accessibility and Global Connectivity:
Digital chess platforms have broken geographical barriers and allowed players from different corners of the world to seamlessly engage in matches. This newfound accessibility supports diverse and challenging environments and exposes players to different play styles and strategies. Mastering the digital chessboard isn't just about moving the pieces on the screen; it is about navigating the vast environment of global competition with inherently honest strategic thinking and adaptability.

2. Analytical Tools and Learning Resources:
Digital chess platforms are equipped with a variety of analytical tools that allow players to accurately analyze their games. Features such as motion

analysis, computer-generated ratings and historical game databases offer invaluable insight into strengths and weaknesses. By actively engaging with these tools, players can improve their strategic and decision-making skills. The digital chessboard thus becomes a dynamic learning space that drives players to continuous improvement.

3. Real Time Feedback and Improvement:
The instant feedback provided by digital platforms is a game changer in skill development. Every move is immediately evaluated, allowing players to measure the effectiveness of their decisions in real time. This immediate feedback loop cultivates a mindset of continuous improvement and encourages players to think about their strategies and quickly correct mistakes. In the field of skill development, this iterative process is essential for improving tactical skills and strategic foresight.

4. Adaptive Challenges and Skill Progression:
Digital chess platforms offer a range of skill-based matchmaking, ensuring that players are constantly challenged at the appropriate level. As players

progress, the difficulty of opponents increases, presenting adaptive challenges that push them beyond their comfort zone. This gradual escalation of difficulty promotes a sense of achievement and motivates players to tackle more complex scenarios. In this context, the digital chessboard acts as a facilitator for continuous skill development.

5. Time management and speed of decision making:

One of the critical aspects of chess is time management. Digital chess platforms introduce time controls that add another layer of complexity to the game. Mastering the digital chessboard requires not only strategic thinking, but also the ability to make quick decisions within a set time frame. This aspect of time management is a transferable skill with off-board applications, making it a valuable asset in a variety of real-world scenarios.

6. Community Engagement and Collaborative Learning:

Digital chess platforms are not just playing arenas; they are thriving communities where players can interact, discuss strategies and learn from each other. Being involved in the chess community enhances the overall learning experience as players share insights, tips and experiences. The digital chessboard thus becomes a virtual classroom where collaborative learning flourishes and the collective knowledge of the community contributes to the development of individual skills.

7. Scenario simulation and training:

Simulations are an integral part of mastering the complexity of chess. Digital platforms allow players to engage in scenario-based training where they can replicate specific positions or practice against specific strategies. This focused approach to training on the digital chessboard allows players to build a repertoire of responses and develop a deeper understanding of the nuances of positions, contributing to a more comprehensive skill set.

8. Development of game dynamics and meta-strategies:

The digital landscape of chess is dynamic, with constant updates and evolving game dynamics. Mastering the digital board requires players to keep up with meta strategies, openings, and trends. This adaptability to the evolving nature of the game instills flexible and strategic thinking. It also encourages players to experiment with different approaches, encouraging creativity and innovation in their game.

9. Artificial Intelligence Integration:

The integration of artificial intelligence (AI) into digital chess platforms adds another layer of complexity and learning. Playing against computer engines of varying skill levels, players are challenged to devise strategies that can outwit AI opponents. This interaction with AI not only improves tactical skills, but also provides insight into algorithmic decision-making, a valuable perspective for players looking to gain a deeper understanding of the game.

10. Life Skills Beyond Chess:

Mastering the digital chessboard goes beyond the realm of the game itself. The skills developed through digital chess – strategic thinking, decision-making under pressure, adaptability and continuous learning, are transferable to various aspects of life. Whether it's academic pursuits, professional endeavors or personal challenges, the cognitive skills honed on the digital board will become the foundation for success in a variety of fields.

The importance of mastering the digital chessboard in skill development cannot be overstated. Accessibility, analytical tools, real-time feedback, adaptive challenges, community engagement, scenario training, evolving game dynamics, AI integration, and life skills cultivated through digital chess all contribute to a holistic learning experience. Embracing the digital dimension of chess not only improves playing ability, but also develops skills that extend far beyond the board, making it a path of constant growth and intellectual enrichment.

Chapter 2. Navigating Digital Chess Platforms

The world of chess has undergone a significant transformation with the advent of digital platforms. Traditional wooden boards and face-to-face matches have been supplemented, if not replaced, by online chess platforms. Navigating these digital realms presents both challenges and opportunities for players looking to master the complexities of the game.

I. Development of chess platforms:

The digitization of chess has brought the game to a global audience and transcends geographic boundaries. The evolution from physical message boards to online platforms has allowed players to connect, compete and learn from each other on a scale never before imagined. As we delve into the complexities of these platforms, understanding their features becomes essential for those looking to hone their skills.

II. Features of digital chess platforms:

A. User Interface and Experience:
Digital platforms offer different interfaces, each designed with unique features. Users can choose an interface that suits their preferences, from minimalistic designs to highly detailed 3D boards. Ease of navigation and visual appeal significantly influence the player's experience, influencing their concentration and strategic thinking during matches.

b. Chess engines and analysis tools:
One of the outstanding features of digital chess platforms is the integration of powerful chess engines. These engines provide real-time analysis, suggest moves and evaluate positions. Players can use this technology to understand their strengths and weaknesses and ultimately improve their strategies and decision-making.

III. Study Resources:

A. Tutorials and Lessons:
Digital platforms often include comprehensive guides and lessons for players of all levels. These resources cover basic chess concepts, opening strategies, tactical motifs, and finishing techniques. Mastering these basics is essential for players who want to build a solid foundation on their chess journey.

b. Riddles and exercises:
Chess platforms offer a variety of puzzles and exercises designed to improve specific skills. Solving tactical puzzles hones the player's ability to spot opportunities, while final exercises improve strategic thinking. Incorporating these drills into regular practice sessions accelerates skill development and promotes a deeper understanding of the game.

IV. Online competitions:

A. Tournaments and Leagues:

Digital platforms facilitate participation in online tournaments and leagues, allowing players to test their skills against opponents from around the world. A competitive environment enhances adaptability, resilience and the ability to handle different playing styles, vital attributes for a well-rounded chess player.

b. Rating systems:

Most platforms implement rating systems that measure a player's skill level. Climbing the ladder through competitive play not only provides a sense of accomplishment, but also ensures that players are constantly challenged. Understanding the nuances of rating systems is essential to setting realistic goals and tracking progress.

V. Digital Chess Challenges:

A. Cheating Concerns:

The anonymity afforded by digital platforms raises concerns about cheating. Players may be tempted to use external assistance or chess engines during games. Addressing this challenge requires robust anti-cheating measures and ethical guidelines to maintain the integrity of online chess.

b. Distraction and fair play:

Gaming on digital platforms brings new distractions such as notifications and other apps. To master the digital chessboard, maintaining focus becomes essential. In addition, ensuring fair play in online competitions requires platforms to implement effective anti-cheating algorithms.

VI. Success Strategy:

A. Organization of time:

Digital chess often involves time controls that require players to make moves within a set time frame. Effective time management is essential as players must balance strategic thinking with quick decision making. Developing a sense of urgency without sacrificing accuracy is a skill that sets successful digital players apart from the rest.

b. Game Analysis:

Post-game analysis is a powerful tool for improvement. Digital platforms allow players to review their plays, identify mistakes and understand alternative moves. Incorporating this analytical approach into everyday practice improves decision-making skills and contributes to overall playing prowess.

VII. Future trends and innovations:

A. Artificial Intelligence Integration:
The future of digital chess platforms may see further integration of artificial intelligence (AI) technologies. Advanced artificial intelligence systems could offer personalized training plans tailored to individual players' strengths and weaknesses. This innovation could revolutionize learning for novice chess enthusiasts.

b. Virtual Reality Chess:
Immersive technologies such as virtual reality (VR) have the potential to redefine the digital chess experience. VR platforms could simulate realistic chess environments, increasing the sense of

presence and involvement. Examining these new trends can give players a glimpse into the future of digital chess.

Navigating digital chess platforms is a dynamic journey that requires a combination of technical prowess and strategic acumen. By leveraging the features of these platforms, aspiring players can turn challenges into opportunities for growth. The evolving landscape of online chess presents a canvas for players to master the digital board and continue to push the boundaries of their skills and understanding of this timeless game.

2.1 Choosing the Right Chess Platform

In the dynamic realm of chess, where tradition meets technology, choosing the right chess platform is crucial for players who want to master the digital board. The rise of online chess platforms has provided players with unprecedented accessibility and opportunities to improve their skills. However, the number of options can be overwhelming. To embark on the journey of digital chess mastery, you need to carefully consider several key factors when choosing the ideal platform.

1. User Interface and Experience:

The cornerstone of a fruitful digital chess experience lies in the platform's user interface and overall experience. A visually intuitive interface coupled with responsive controls can greatly influence the way players react to a game. Look for platforms that offer a seamless and aesthetically pleasing design, ensuring a smooth transition from traditional to digital chess.

2. Skill Level and Learning Resources:

Different platforms cater to different skill levels, from beginners to grandmasters. Choosing a platform that matches your current skill level will ensure a challenging but enjoyable experience. In addition, a comprehensive set of learning resources, including tutorials, puzzles, and commented games, can contribute immensely to your chess education. Choose a platform that supports continuous learning and skill development.

3. Community and competition:

Chess is not just a game; it's a community. With an active and engaging user community, the platform provides opportunities for social interaction, friendly games and even mentorship. In addition, strong competition is key to growth. Choose a platform that hosts regular tournaments, leagues and matchmaking features to test your skills against a variety of opponents.

4. Game Analysis and Review Tools:

The digital frontier offers unrivaled analytical tools for chess enthusiasts. Choose a platform that provides in-depth game analysis, including turn-by-turn breakdowns, performance statistics and computer-generated ratings. These qualities are invaluable for understanding mistakes, identifying patterns, and honing strategic thinking.

5. Compatibility and Availability:

Consider the compatibility of the platform with different devices and operating systems. A platform that seamlessly transitions from desktop to mobile device ensures that you can practice and play chess wherever you are. Accessibility features such as offline play can be useful for times when an internet connection is not available.

6. Fair Play and Safety Precautions:
Maintaining a fair and safe playing environment is paramount in the digital chess environment. Explore the platform's fair play, anti-cheat and account security policies. Platforms with robust monitoring systems and penalties for unethical behavior contribute to a more enjoyable and trustworthy chess experience.

7. Pricing and Subscription Models:
While many chess platforms offer free access, some features may be restricted to premium subscribers. Evaluate the platform's subscription models, pricing tiers and the value they provide. Consider your budget and the specific features that match your learning and gaming preferences.

8. Different Game Modes:

Chess is a game of endless possibilities, and a platform that offers different game modes adds depth to the experience. Whether it's classic games, speed chess or unique variations, the variety of options keeps the game fresh and exciting.

9. Platform Update and Support:

The platform's commitment to regular updates and ongoing support is testament to its commitment to user satisfaction. Look for a platform that actively listens to user feedback, quickly resolves issues, and introduces new features to improve the overall experience.

10. Reviews and Recommendations:

Before committing to a particular platform, research reviews and seek recommendations from other chess enthusiasts. Learning from the experiences of others can provide valuable insights into the strengths and weaknesses of different platforms.

mastering the digital chessboard requires careful consideration in choosing the right platform. By assessing factors such as user interface, skill level support, community engagement, analytics tools, availability, fair play measures, cost, game modes, platform support and user reviews, players can make an informed choice that aligns with their goals and preferences . The digital chess realm is rich with opportunity, and choosing the right platform is the first step to a fulfilling and rewarding chess journey.

2.2 Understanding User Interfaces and Features

User interfaces (UI) and features play a key role in mastering the digital chessboard, providing players with a dynamic and immersive experience. In the realm of chess, where strategic thinking and precision are paramount, a well-designed user interface coupled with thoughtful features can greatly improve overall gameplay and help the player master the digital board.

The user interface acts as a gateway between the player and the digital chessboard and includes visuals, controls and interactions that facilitate a seamless gaming experience. An intuitive and user-friendly user interface is essential, allowing players to focus on strategic moves rather than struggling with a complex interface. Chess platforms often use a clean and minimalist design, presenting the board and pieces in a clear and easy-to-understand manner.

One of the key aspects of an effective digital chess user interface is responsiveness. The responsive user interface ensures that player inputs are instantly reflected on the board, eliminating any lag that could disrupt the flow of gameplay. Whether it's dragging pieces or making a move by clicking, the user interface should respond instantly to the player's actions, mimicking the real tactile experience of traditional chess.

In addition, customization options within the user interface allow players to tailor the board to their preferences. Customizable themes, tile styles, and board colors not only add a personal touch, but also contribute to a visually comfortable environment for extended gaming sessions. This level of personalization promotes a sense of ownership of the digital chessboard, making the gaming experience more enjoyable and engaging.

In addition to the user interface, the features integrated into the digital chess platform are essential to enhance the overall experience. Chess enthusiasts often appreciate platforms that offer a variety of game modes, including standard games, puzzles, and online multiplayer options. A variety of game modes suit different skill levels and preferences, providing both novice and experienced players with ways to improve and have fun.

A key feature that helps in mastering the digital chessboard is the analysis tool. This tool allows players to review and analyze their games, identifying strengths and weaknesses and missed opportunities. By delving into the intricacies of each move, players can refine their strategies, learn from their mistakes, and gradually improve their overall chess skills. The ability to revisit past games and learn from them is a powerful tool for improvement that a well-designed digital platform should offer.

In addition to the analytical tools, a comprehensive tutorial or tutorial section is also invaluable for players looking to improve their skills. Whether it's understanding advanced tactics, mastering opening strategies, or mastering endgame scenarios, the digital chess platform should provide educational resources to satisfy players of all skill levels. This educational component contributes significantly to the mastery of the digital chessboard and supports a community of continuous learning and improvement.

Social elements also play a vital role in the digital chess experience. Online multiplayer modes, chat functions and the ability to challenge friends create a vibrant community of chess enthusiasts. Engaging other players, sharing strategies and participating in tournaments contributes to a dynamic and rewarding gaming environment. The sense of competition and camaraderie within the digital chess community adds another layer of motivation for players trying to master the intricacies of the game.

Additionally, a robust digital chess platform should include features that include technological advancements such as artificial intelligence (AI) opponents. AI-powered chess engines provide players with challenging and adaptive opponents, allowing them to test their skills against sophisticated algorithms. Playing against AI opponents is an effective way to simulate real-game scenarios, improving strategic thinking and decision-making skills in a controlled environment.

Mastering the digital chessboard is a multifaceted journey that largely depends on user interface design and thoughtful integration of features within the digital platform. An intuitive and responsive user interface along with customization options sets the stage for an immersive gaming experience. Features such as analytics tools, tutorials and social interactions add to the player's learning curve and overall enjoyment. By understanding and harnessing the potential of user interfaces and features, chess enthusiasts can embark on a fulfilling journey to mastery in the digital realm.

2.3 Setting Up and Customizing Your Digital Chess Environment

Mastering the game of chess goes beyond moving pieces on a physical board; the digital realm opens up a world of possibilities for chess enthusiasts. In this comprehensive guide, we delve into the art of setting up and customizing your digital chess environment. From choosing the right platform to personalized aesthetics, embark on a journey that will not only improve your skills, but transform your chess experience into a custom masterpiece.

Choosing the Perfect Chess Platform:

The foundation of your digital chess journey begins with choosing the right platform. Whether you opt for popular online chess sites like Chess.com or adopt stand-alone apps like lichess, each platform has its own unique features and community. Dive into the nuances, explore the user interfaces and find a virtual arena that resonates with your play style.

Customizing the Virtual Chessboard:

Customizing the digital board to your preferences can greatly improve your overall gaming experience. Adjusting the color of the board, the style of the figures, and even the background can create a visually pleasing atmosphere that contributes to concentration. Strike a balance between aesthetics and functionality and transform the virtual chessboard into your customized battlefield.

Exploring Chess Engines and Analysis Tools:
Take your game to the next level by integrating powerful chess engines and analytical tools into your digital environment. Platforms like Stockfish and Komodo offer unparalleled analytics, providing insight into your movements and suggesting improvements. Dive into the settings, tweak the engine parameters and witness the magic as your game evolves.

Mastering the Art of Opening Databases:
Unravel the secrets of famous chess openings with the digital databases at your disposal. Platforms like ChessBase contain a large collection of games that allow you to explore different openings, study grandmaster strategies, and improve your repertoire. Customizable filters allow you to

customize your search and provide personalized learning.

Adoption of online chess communities:

The digital chess world thrives on community engagement. Joining online chess communities will introduce you to a diverse range of players, each with a unique playing style. Participate in forums, discuss strategies and challenge opponents to friendly matches. The synergy of collective knowledge and shared passion elevates your journey from mere play to a dynamic chess experience.

Optimizing digital chess settings:

Tune your digital chess environment by optimizing your hardware and software settings. Ensure a seamless experience by adjusting display settings, optimizing mouse sensitivity, and exploring keyboard shortcuts. A well-optimized setup will not only improve your game, but also contribute to a more fun and efficient digital chess experience.

Balancing aesthetics and functionality:

Find a harmonious balance between aesthetics and functionality when customizing your digital chess environment. Experiment with different themes, parts sets and background images and prefer a clean and uncluttered interface. Let your digital chessboard reflect your unique style without compromising the clarity of the game.

In the digital realm, mastering the chessboard goes hand in hand with creating a personalized and optimized environment. From choosing the right platform to fine-tuning every aspect of your setup, this guide will set you on a journey where strategy meets style. Elevate your chess experience, embrace the digital frontier, and watch your mastery of the game flourish in a world of endless possibilities.

Chapter 3. Strategic and Tactical Insights

In the rapidly evolving digital landscape, mastering the complexity of the "digital chessboard" is essential for both individuals and businesses. This metaphorical chessboard represents the dynamic and ever-evolving nature of the digital world, where strategic and tactical insights play a key role in achieving success. In this exploration, we'll delve into the importance of strategic thinking and tactical maneuvers and clarify how they work synergistically to navigate the complexities of the digital realm.

I. Understanding the Digital Chessboard:

A. Dynamics of the digital landscape:
The digital landscape is characterized by rapid progress, constant innovation and a myriad of interconnected elements. It is similar to a vast

chessboard, where each move affects the overall landscape. Strategic thinking involves understanding these dynamics, identifying key players and anticipating their moves.

B. Interplay of strategy and tactics:
While strategy and tactics are often used interchangeably, it is important to distinguish them. Strategy involves setting long-term goals and outlining an overarching plan to achieve them. Tactics, on the other hand, are the specific actions taken to execute the strategy. On the digital chessboard, effective coordination of both is essential for success.

II. Strategic Insights in the Digital Realm:

A. Defining clear goals:
On the digital chessboard, well-defined goals are the cornerstone of a successful strategy. Whether it's market expansion, branding or technological innovation, clear goals enable a strategic plan for navigating the digital landscape.

B. Adaptive Planning:

Given the dynamic nature of the digital realm, rigid strategic plans can prove ineffective. Adaptive planning involves constantly reassessing and adapting strategies based on new trends, technological shifts, and evolving consumer behavior.

C. Competitive Intelligence:

Understanding your competitors' moves is analogous to anticipating your opponent's chess moves. Strategic insights in the digital realm require a thorough awareness of competitor activities, market positioning and emerging threats to proactively position ourselves for success.

III. Tactical Mastery on the Digital Chessboard:

A. Agility in Execution:

Tactical maneuvers in the digital landscape require agility and quick decision-making. The ability to quickly adapt tactics in response to real-time data and changing circumstances is critical to staying ahead of the game.

B. Data-Based Decision Making:

Insights-based tactics provide competitive advantage on the digital board. Leveraging analytics, artificial intelligence, and other tools helps make informed decisions, optimize campaigns, and maximize ROI.

C. Seamless technology integration:

On the digital chessboard, the use of new technologies is a tactical move that can bring significant benefits. Whether integrating AI, blockchain, or immersive technologies, strategically incorporating these tools increases tactical effectiveness.

IV. Synergizing strategies and tactics:

A. Alignment for cohesive design:

To successfully master the digital chessboard, there must be a seamless alignment of strategic goals and tactical execution. This coherence ensures that each tactical move contributes to the overarching strategic goals.

B. Iterative feedback loops:

Creating iterative feedback loops between strategy and tactics facilitates continuous improvement. Insights gained from tactical execution can inform and refine strategic planning, creating a dynamic cycle of improvement and adaptation.

C. Balancing short-term gains with a long-term vision:

While tactical maneuvers are often associated with short-term gains, it is essential to ensure that they are aligned with a long-term strategic vision. Finding the right balance between immediate wins and sustainable growth is the hallmark of mastering the digital chessboard.

In an ever-evolving digital environment, mastering the digital chessboard requires a holistic approach that combines strategic thinking with tactical agility. As individuals and businesses navigate this complex terrain, the ability to adapt, innovate and strategically position themselves becomes paramount. By understanding the dynamics of the digital chessboard and combining strategic insights with tactical mastery, one can not only survive, but thrive in the dynamic world of the digital era.

3.1 Adapting Traditional Strategies to Digital Chess

Adapting traditional chess strategies to the digital realm is a crucial aspect of mastering the board nowadays. As technology continues to shape our world, the game of chess is not exempt from its transformative influence. In this survey, we delve into the intricacies of merging ancient chess principles with the dynamics of the digital board and provide insight into how players can elevate their game in the virtual arena.

1. Opening repertoire in the digital landscape*

One of the basic areas of adaptation is the opening repertoire. Traditional openings that have proven themselves on physical boards may require adjustments in the digital realm. Understanding how specific openings translate to a digital board is essential given the nuances of online platforms. Factors such as time controls, opponent tendencies, and the dominance of certain lines online can affect the effectiveness of traditional openings.

2. Time management and clock awareness

In the field of digital chess, time management takes on a new level of importance. Clock awareness is paramount and players must adapt their strategies to the faster pace of online games. Techniques such as pre-movement and the use of increments become essential skills to be mastered. Balancing strategic depth and efficient use of time is a delicate art that distinguishes successful digital players.

3. Positive understanding in the digital domain

Maintaining a strong positional understanding remains the cornerstone of success in both traditional and digital chess. However, the visualization of the positions may be different on the digital board. Players must adapt their spatial perception to the screen and ensure a smooth transition between the mental representation of the position and its representation on the digital board. This adjustment is essential for accurate assessments and strategic decisions.

4. Opponent Online Behavior Customization

In traditional chess, players often rely on visual cues and body language to infer their opponent's intentions. In the digital realm, these cues are absent, requiring a shift in focus toward interpreting online behavior. Recognizing patterns in opponent movements, time management, and psychological tendencies can provide a strategic advantage. Adapting to the nuances of online interactions adds another layer of complexity to the game.

5. Using Online Resources for Improvement

The digital age offers a wealth of online resources for chess improvement. Players can access extensive databases, participate in virtual training sessions and analyze games using powerful engines. Adapting traditional learning methods to utilize these resources is essential to mastering the digital board. Integrating technology-enabled learning into a training regimen can accelerate skill development.

6. Managing Digital Distraction

Unlike the peaceful atmosphere of a traditional chess tournament, playing online exposes players to a myriad of distractions. Adapting to these distractions is essential to maintaining focus at critical moments. Strategies for minimizing interruptions, creating a favorable gaming environment, and managing external factors are becoming an integral part of the player's digital toolkit.

7. Evolving Endgame Techniques

Endgames, often considered the soul of chess, are undergoing a transformation in the digital landscape. Techniques that were effective on physical boards may require modifications due to the calculation accuracy of online engines. Players must adapt their endgame strategies to incorporate digital insights while maintaining the timeless principles that govern the endgame.

The journey of adapting traditional strategies to the digital chessboard is a constant process of evolution and refinement. Embracing the unique challenges and opportunities presented by the digital realm is essential for players who want to master the complexities of online chess. By combining the wisdom of traditional chess principles with the adaptability required in the digital age, players can navigate the virtual chessboard with confidence and strategic prowess.

3.2 Exploiting Digital Tools for Tactical Advantage

In the ever-evolving landscape of the digital age, mastering the art of navigating the digital chessboard has become a necessity for individuals and businesses alike. Strategic use of digital tools can be the key to gaining a tactical advantage in this dynamic environment. In this survey, we delve into the ways in which the use of digital tools can improve decision-making, optimize performance and ultimately lead to digital success.

Understanding the Digital Chessboard:

The term "digital checkerboard" aptly describes the complex and strategic nature of the current landscape. Like a game of chess where every move has consequences, decisions made in the digital realm are reflected across platforms and channels. To master this virtual chessboard, you must first understand the multifaceted layers of the digital landscape, including social media, data analytics, artificial intelligence, and more.

Strategic decision making with data analysis:

The key to mastering the digital chessboard is the ability to harness the power of data analysis. Thanks to the huge amount of data generated daily, organizations can gain valuable insights into consumer behavior, market trends and competitor strategies. By leveraging advanced analytics tools, businesses can make informed decisions, identify patterns and predict future trends. This strategic use of data analytics provides a clear advantage in navigating the digital landscape.

Performance Optimization with Artificial Intelligence:

Artificial Intelligence (AI) serves as a formidable ally in the quest to dominate the digital chessboard. From personalized customer experiences to predictive analytics, AI algorithms increase efficiency and accuracy. By automating routine tasks and offering real-time insights, businesses can optimize their performance, adapt quickly to change, and stay ahead of the competition. The strategic integration of artificial intelligence into digital strategies enables organizations to make proactive moves on the virtual chessboard.

Improving communication through social networks:

Social media platforms have emerged as key arenas in the digital chess game. Strategic use of these platforms can significantly impact brand visibility, customer engagement and competitive position. Organizations that understand the nuances of social media dynamics can use these channels to spread information, build relationships, and even influence public perception. Effective social media management is becoming a tactical advantage in an increasingly connected digital ecosystem.

Cyber Security as a Knight in Shining Armor:

As the digital environment expands, the importance of cyber security cannot be overstated. Protecting sensitive information and protecting against cyber threats are paramount to mastering the digital chessboard. Organizations that prioritize cyber security not only protect themselves from potential attacks, but also gain the trust of their stakeholders. Cybersecurity serves as the knight in shining armor to fend off invisible threats and ensure the longevity of digital strategies.

Success Strategy:

Mastering the digital chessboard requires a combination of strategic planning, adaptability and constant learning. Businesses and individuals should take a holistic approach and incorporate various digital tools and technologies into their arsenal. In addition, staying up-to-date on new trends and innovations is critical to maintaining a competitive edge. Flexibility in strategy and willingness to experiment with new tools are key attributes of successful digital players.

In the ever-changing landscape of the digital age, the ability to use digital tools to tactical advantage is a prerequisite for success. Understanding the nuances of the digital chessboard, integrating data analytics, leveraging artificial intelligence, mastering social media, and prioritizing cybersecurity are essential components of a winning strategy. As individuals and organizations navigate this complex environment, mastering the digital chessboard becomes a powerful tool for achieving goals, overcoming adversaries, and ensuring sustained success in the dynamic world of the digital age.

3.3 Analyzing and Learning from Digital Games

In the field of strategic thinking and cognitive skills, digital chess stands as a timeless bastion. With the advent of technology, the traditional chessboard has transformed into a digital interface that has created new opportunities for players to hone their skills. This development has given rise to a fascinating intersection between chess and digital games, and presents a unique opportunity for enthusiasts to delve into the intricacies of the game. Analyzing and learning from digital games becomes a pivotal aspect in mastering the digital board, providing insight into strategy, pattern recognition and adaptive thinking.

One of the key benefits of engaging with digital chess platforms is the amount of data they generate. Every move, every decision and every play is recorded, giving players a vast database to analyze their performance. This data-driven approach allows players to identify patterns in their play, understand common pitfalls, and refine their strategies. The ability to review past games and learn from them serves as a valuable tool in the arsenal of a chess player seeking to improve.

In addition, digital chess platforms often contain sophisticated algorithms and artificial intelligence, allowing players to face virtual opponents of varying skill levels. This dynamic environment provides a diverse and challenging training ground that forces players to adapt and develop their strategies. The adaptive nature of digital opponents encourages resilience and the development of a versatile playstyle, which are key elements to mastering the ever-changing digital chessboard.

Integrating tutorials and interactive lessons within digital chess platforms enhances the learning experience. These features offer players insight into basic chess principles, advanced tactics, and strategic nuances. Whether you are a beginner or an experienced player, the availability of structured lessons provides a systematic approach to skill development. Players can immerse themselves in specific aspects of the game, from opening to endgames, gradually gaining a comprehensive understanding of chess strategy.

In addition to structured lessons, the community aspect of digital chess platforms contributes significantly to the learning process. Players can engage in discussions, share insights and even participate in virtual tournaments. The exchange of ideas within the community fosters a collaborative learning environment where players can benefit from the collective wisdom of their peers. This social dimension adds a dynamic layer to the lessons and creates a sense of camaraderie among chess enthusiasts moving around the digital board.

An interesting aspect of digital chess is the integration of computer analysis tools. These tools provide real-time assessment of positions, suggest optimal moves and highlight mistakes. While reliance on such tools raises ethical questions in competitive play, they undeniably serve as powerful learning aids. Players can use computer analysis to dissect their plays and gain a deeper understanding of strategic subtleties and tactical nuances that they may have missed during the game.

The transition from physical to digital chessboards also introduces the concept of gamification. Many digital platforms include elements of gamification to make the learning process more engaging and fun. Achievements, leaderboards and rewards add a layer of motivation and encourage players to invest time and effort into their chess journey. This gamified approach not only enhances the learning experience, but also contributes to the development of a growth mindset – essential qualities for those who want to master the digital chessboard.

In addition to the wealth of resources available on digital platforms, the availability of online chess communities and tutorials also democratizes the learning process. Regardless of geographic location or time constraints, players can immerse themselves in the world of chess, connect with fellow enthusiasts, and access a wealth of educational materials. This accessibility played a key role in the widespread popularity and resurgence of interest in chess, overcoming traditional barriers to entry.

However, it is crucial to recognize the potential pitfalls of relying solely on digital platforms for learning chess. The lack of face-to-face interaction and the tactile feel of physical pieces can detract from a holistic chess experience. Achieving a balance between digital and traditional forms of chess provides a well-rounded skill set that combines the analytical benefits of digital platforms with the tangible and social aspects of the physical game.

Analyzing and learning from digital games offers chess enthusiasts a multifaceted approach to mastering the digital chessboard. The integration of data analytics, artificial intelligence, tutorials, community engagement and gamification together contribute to a rich learning environment. Embracing the advantages of digital platforms while being mindful of potential disadvantages allows players to navigate the intricate world of chess, honing their skills and strategy in pursuit of mastery on the digital board.

Chapter 4. Mastering Online Chess Etiquette and Community

Mastering online chess etiquette and community engagement is essential for those who want to excel on the digital board. In the world of online chess, players not only compete against each other, but also become part of a global community. This article explores the intricacies of online chess etiquette and highlights the importance of good sportsmanship, fair play and effective communication. In addition, it delves into the dynamics of the online chess community, providing insight into building connections, participating in tournaments, and using online resources to improve skills.

Understanding Online Chess Etiquette:

Online chess etiquette is a set of unwritten rules that govern player behavior during games. Practicing proper etiquette not only shows respect for your opponents, but also contributes to a positive online chess environment. Here are some key aspects of mastering online chess etiquette:

1. Respect your opponent's time:

   - Avoid unnecessary delays and think about your moves during your opponent's turn.

   - If you need to leave the game temporarily, use the appropriate functions to signal a pause or resignation.

2. Avoid unsportsmanlike conduct:

   - Avoid using disrespectful language, taunts or any form of unsportsmanlike conduct.

   - Remember that there is a real person behind every username; treat them with courtesy and respect.

3. Use chat wisely:

- Keep in mind the chat feature; use it to greet an opponent or discuss the game, but avoid any abusive language.
- If your opponent prefers a quiet game, respect his choice and keep chat to a minimum.

4. Fair Play:
- Resist the temptation to use external help or computer engines during games.
- Follow the principles of fair play and enjoy the game for its intellectual challenge.

Building Positive Community Engagement:
Beyond individual games, the online chess community offers plenty of opportunities for players to connect, learn, and grow together. Here are ways to get positively involved in the online chess community:

1. Join Chess Forums and Communities:
- Participate in online chess forums to share experiences, ask questions and learn from others.
- Engage in discussions about strategy, tactics and notable chess games.

2. Online chess clubs and tournaments:

   - Join online chess clubs or communities that match your skill level and interests.

   - Participate in online tournaments to challenge yourself and meet other enthusiasts.

3. Respect your opponent and learn from defeats:

   - Whether you win or lose, maintain a respectful attitude towards your opponents.

   - Use defeats as learning opportunities; analyze your games and seek advice from stronger players.

4. Contribute to the community:

   - Share your knowledge by creating chess content such as analysis videos or articles.

   - Offer to help other players, especially those new to the online chess scene.

Using online resources to improve skills:
Mastering the digital chessboard goes beyond just playing games; it involves continuous learning and improvement. Here's how to make the most of online resources to improve your skills:

1. Chess Learning Platforms:
   - Explore online chess learning platforms that offer lessons, puzzles and interactive tutorials.
   - Use features like computer analysis to understand your mistakes and areas for improvement.

2. Online chess databases:
   - Access online chess databases to study games played by grandmasters and top players.
   - Analyze different openings, middle game strategies and end games to expand your chess knowledge.

3. Join Chess Software:
   - Use chess software for practice games, analysis and building your opening repertoire.
   - Stay up to date with the latest developments in chess theory and use the software to stay ahead of evolving strategies.

4. Connect with Chess Trainers:

- Consider hiring an online chess coach for personalized advice and feedback.

- Work on specific aspects of your game with a coach and focus on areas for improvement.

Mastering online chess etiquette and community engagement is integral to excellence in the digital chessboard environment. By cultivating good sportsmanship, actively participating in the online chess community, and using available resources to improve skills, players can not only improve their game, but also make a positive contribution to the wider chess community.

4.1 Code of Conduct in Digital Chess

Mastering the digital chessboard involves not only honing your skills, but also following a code of conduct that promotes a positive and respectful environment. In the realm of online chess, where players connect virtually, the following principles are essential for an enjoyable and fair gaming experience.

1. Respect your opponent:

Treat your opponents with courtesy and sportsmanship. Avoid disrespectful comments or behavior and remember that behind every username is a real person trying to improve their skills.

2. Fair Play:

Follow the principles of fair play. Do not use external help, chess tools or consult with others during the game. Honesty is paramount to maintaining the integrity of the game.

3. Timeliness:

Follow the agreed time controls and avoid unnecessary delays. Respect your opponent's time by making quick moves, which makes for a smoother and more enjoyable game experience for both players.

4. No Cheating:

Cheating undermines the spirit of the game. Avoid any form of cheating, including using chess tools, databases, or accepting help from others during the game. Fair competition is essential for personal growth and the chess community as a whole.

5. Avoid unsportsmanlike conduct:

Conduct yourself in a manner that reflects the values of sportsmanship. Avoid mocking, mocking, or any behavior that could be considered offensive. A positive and respectful attitude contributes to a healthier chess community.

6. Learn from defeats:

Accept losses as opportunities to improve. Instead of expressing frustration or guilt, use defeats as an opportunity to analyze and improve your skills. Constructive criticism and self-reflection are essential components of mastering the digital chessboard.

7. Community Engagement:

Contribute positively to the online chess community. Share knowledge, insights and experiences with other players. Foster a supportive atmosphere that fosters learning and collaboration.

8. Report foul play:

If you suspect foul play or witness a violation of the rules, report it to the relevant platform or tournament organizers. Maintaining a clean and fair environment depends on community vigilance.

9. Watch your language:

Use respectful and appropriate language in chat or messages. Avoid offensive or inflammatory comments and promote a more inclusive and welcoming digital chess community.

10. Continuous Improvement:

Strive to continually improve both your chess skills and adherence to the code of conduct. Review these principles regularly and think about how you can contribute to a positive and fair online chess environment.

By adopting these principles, chess players can not only improve their skills on the digital board, but also help create a respectful and fun online chess community.

4.2 Building a Positive Online Chess Presence

In the age of digital connectivity, chess enthusiasts have embraced online platforms as a means to hone their skills and engage in exciting matches with opponents from around the world. However, beyond strategic moves on the virtual chessboard, there is a crucial aspect that players often overlook – building a positive online chess presence. As in traditional chess, where etiquette and sportsmanship play a vital role, the digital realm requires a set of guidelines to foster a respectful and welcoming community. This article explores the importance of cultivating a positive online chess presence and offers practical tips for navigating the complexities of the digital chessboard.

1. Respectful Communication:
Effective communication is the cornerstone of any positive online presence. In the world of online chess, this means respectful and sportsmanship. Whether you win or lose, maintaining a kind attitude promotes a healthy gaming environment. Avoiding

negative comments, trash talk or unsportsmanlike behavior makes for a more enjoyable experience for all involved.

2. Learning from defeats:

Chess is a game of constant learning, and defeats are inevitable milestones on the road to improvement. Instead of getting frustrated after a loss, see it as an opportunity to analyze your mistakes and learn from them. Engaging in post-match analysis, seeking feedback from stronger players, and reviewing your own moves will not only improve your skills, but also contribute positively to the online chess community.

3. Encourage Community Engagement:

Active participation in the online chess community goes beyond just playing games. Joining forums, newsgroups or chess clubs can provide valuable insights, foster camaraderie and contribute to community growth. Sharing your experiences, discussing strategies and celebrating successes with other players creates a sense of unity that reinforces the positive fabric of the digital chess world.

4. Acceptance of Fair Play:

Maintaining fair play is the foundation of a positive online chess presence. Avoid using chess engines or other external help during the game, as this not only undermines the integrity of the match, but also damages your reputation within the community. Adherence to the principles of fair play not only ensures a level playing field, but also contributes to a more trustworthy and fun online chess environment.

5. Constructive Feedback:

Giving and receiving constructive feedback is a two-way street in the online chess community. When offering advice or suggestions to other players, focus on constructive and useful insights rather than criticizing mistakes. Likewise, be open to receiving feedback from others and use it as a tool for improvement rather than taking it personally. This reciprocal approach fosters a supportive atmosphere that encourages growth and development.

6. Respecting time controls:

Online chess often involves a variety of time controls, from blitz games to classic games. Respecting the agreed time controls is essential for a positive gaming experience. Avoid time-wasting tactics such as purposeful delays or excessive pauses, which can lead to frustration for both players. Complying with time controls demonstrates good sportsmanship and contributes to a smoother and more enjoyable gaming environment.

7. Mindful use of chat and emotes:

Many online chess platforms allow players to chat or use emotes during the game. It is essential to use these functions with care and to avoid any form of disrespect or distraction. Instead, use chat to exchange pleasantries, discuss the game (without revealing strategies), or express admiration for a well-played move. Emotes, when used sparingly, can add a touch of sportsmanship to the overall gaming experience.

Building a positive online chess presence isn't just about mastering the digital chessboard; it's about creating a friendly and respectful community for players of all skill levels. By following the principles of good sportsmanship, fair play and constructive engagement, chess enthusiasts can contribute to a thriving online environment that supports learning, growth and fun. As you navigate the complexities of the digital chess world, remember that behind every username is a fellow chess lover, and together we can elevate the online chess experience for everyone.

4.3 Participating in Tournaments and Online Chess Communities

In the dynamic environment of chess, the digital chessboard has become an area where enthusiasts converge to hone their skills, engage in strategic battles, and build a sense of community. The transition from traditional chessboards to a digital interface has opened up new avenues for players to explore and elevate their game. This article discusses the importance of participating in tournaments and engaging in online chess communities as an integral part of mastering the digital chessboard.

Digital Chess Revolution:

The advent of digital technology has revolutionized the way chess is played and experienced. Digital chessboards offer convenience, accessibility and a plethora of features that enhance the overall gaming experience. Whether you're a seasoned player or a newcomer, moving to a digital platform provides a gateway to a vast world of opportunities.

Tournaments: Test Base for Championships:

Participation in online chess tournaments serves as an essential testing ground for novice players. Ranging from local competitions to international championships, these tournaments provide a diverse group of opponents, each with unique play styles and strategies. The digital format allows players to engage in matches against competitors from different corners of the world, promoting exposure to different approaches to the game.

Tournament Dynamics: Learning Through Competition:

Competing in tournaments improves analytical and strategic skills. Faced with a diverse array of opponents, it challenges players to adapt and evolve their game. Each match becomes a lesson, an opportunity to understand different openings, tactics and endgame scenarios. Constant exposure to different playing styles is like a chess classroom where you learn not only from wins but also from losses.

Pressure and Power: Mimicking Real Chess:

Tournaments simulate the pressure and intensity of chess chess, which contributes to the development of mental strength. Dealing with time constraints, dealing with the psychological impact of wins and losses, and making critical decisions under pressure are skills that players develop through tournament experience. Mastering these aspects is just as essential in the digital realm as it is on the physical board.

Online Chess Communities: Building a Digital Chess Ecosystem:

Outside of the competitive arena, online chess communities play a key role in the journey to mastery of the digital chessboard. These communities act as hubs where players, regardless of skill level, converge to share knowledge, seek advice, and foster a sense of camaraderie.

Knowledge exchange: a collective learning experience:

Joining online chess communities facilitates a rich exchange of knowledge. Players discuss strategies, analyze games, and seek advice on specific chess principles. The collective wisdom of the community becomes a valuable resource for improving your understanding of the game. From opening theory to complex endgames, the community serves as a repository of insights that contribute to overall improvement.

Coaching and Mentoring: Digital Consulting:

Many online chess communities offer coaching and mentoring programs that connect players with experienced mentors. These digital guides provide personalized feedback, tailored training plans and strategic advice. The mentor-student relationship thrives in the digital realm, transcending geographic boundaries and allowing players to receive advice from seasoned experts, further accelerating their progress.

Chess variants and specialized communities:
The digital platform also facilitates the exploration of chess variants and specialized communities. Whether it's blitz, bullet or themed tournaments, players can dive into specific areas of interest. This diversification not only keeps the game engaging, but also allows players to develop a broader understanding of chess dynamics.

Crossroads of Tournaments and Communities:
In the synergy between participating in tournaments and engaging in online chess communities, true mastery of the digital chessboard unfolds. Tournaments provide practical application of skills learned within the community, while the community

serves as a constant source of improvement and learning between tournaments.

Post-Tournament Analysis: Community Feedback:
After participating in a tournament, players often turn to online communities for post-match analysis. Sharing games, discussing critical positions and seeking feedback from colleagues contributes to a deeper understanding of one's own strengths and weaknesses. This iterative process of playing, analyzing and learning is essential to the continuous improvement of a player's game.

Community Organized Tournaments: A Unique Experience:
Some online chess communities organize their own tournaments, promoting a sense of camaraderie among participants. These events often have a unique flavor, with members competing in an environment that combines friendly competition with a shared passion for the game. Community organized tournaments create a bridge between the virtual and real worlds and enhance the overall chess experience.

A Holistic Approach to Mastery:

Mastering the digital chessboard is not a solitary pursuit, but a journey enriched by the intersection of tournaments and online chess communities. Tournaments provide a crucible for testing and honing skills, while communities offer an environment for constant learning and growth. Embracing both aspects creates a holistic approach to chess mastery where the digital realm becomes a living ecosystem for players to thrive, connect and improve their game.

Conclusion

Mastering the digital chessboard is a journey that goes beyond mere moves on the screen; it's a pursuit that delves into the realms of strategy, foresight, and adaptability. At the end of this survey, it is clear that the fusion of traditional chess principles with digital advances has redefined the landscape of the game. A digital chessboard is not just a virtual replica; it is a dynamic arena that requires a fine understanding of both chess theory and technological intricacies.

At the heart of this conclusion is the recognition of the profound impact of technology on chess. The shift from wooden boards to digital interfaces not only facilitated global connectivity, but also revolutionized the way players approached the game. Mastering the digital chessboard requires a synthesis of timeless chess wisdom with the tools and knowledge that technology offers.

One of the key aspects of this mastery is the use of chess engines. These powerful algorithms have become indispensable companions for players looking to improve. The ability to utilize the analytical capabilities of the engines while maintaining the creativity and intuition inherent in human play is what sets the modern chess master apart. The bottom line is that harmonious cooperation between human intellect and artificial intelligence is the key to unlocking new dimensions of understanding on the digital chessboard.

In addition, the development of online platforms has democratized access to chess education. The conclusion is not just about mastering the moves, but about embracing the communal nature of the chess community. Forums, online tournaments, and shared learning experiences have turned the solitary pursuit of chess mastery into a shared activity. The digital chessboard is therefore a symbol of connected minds that transcend geographical boundaries.

As we delve deeper into the conclusion, the importance of adaptability in the digital age becomes apparent. The speed of information dissemination and the constant development of chess theory require a flexible and open approach.

Mastering the digital chessboard is not a static achievement, but an ongoing process of adaptation and refinement. This conclusion underscores the importance of remaining attuned to the dynamic nature of chess in the digital era.

Moreover, in this conclusion, the psychological aspects of the game come to the fore. The digital chessboard, with its anonymity and global player base, introduces new dimensions to psychological warfare. The ability to navigate the complexities of online interactions, effectively manage time pressure, and maintain mental composure in the face of adversity is proving to be a critical aspect of mastering the digital chessboard. This conclusion summarizes the need for a holistic approach that includes both the board and the mind.

A crucial aspect of this conclusion revolves around ethical considerations in the field of digital chess. The advent of sophisticated cheating methods poses challenges to the integrity of the game. The conclusion therefore emphasizes the importance of fair play, honesty and adherence to ethical standards. Mastering the digital chessboard is not just about outsmarting your opponent, but doing it with honor and respect for the game.

The journey to mastering the digital chessboard is a multi-faceted expedition that goes beyond the boundaries of the traditional game. It is a synergy of classical chess principles with the transformative capabilities of technology. The conclusion from this survey is that a successful chess master in the digital age is one who can seamlessly integrate human intuition with the analytical power of engines, navigate the psychological nuances of online play, adapt to the ever-evolving chess environment, and uphold the game's ethical standards. The digital chessboard is not just a platform for moves; it is a dynamic arena where intellect, adaptability and sportsmanship converge to redefine the essence of chess mastery.